The Back Way To Normal
by Allin KHG

2016 KHG InterServ
empallin@yahoo.com
Oklahoma City, OK

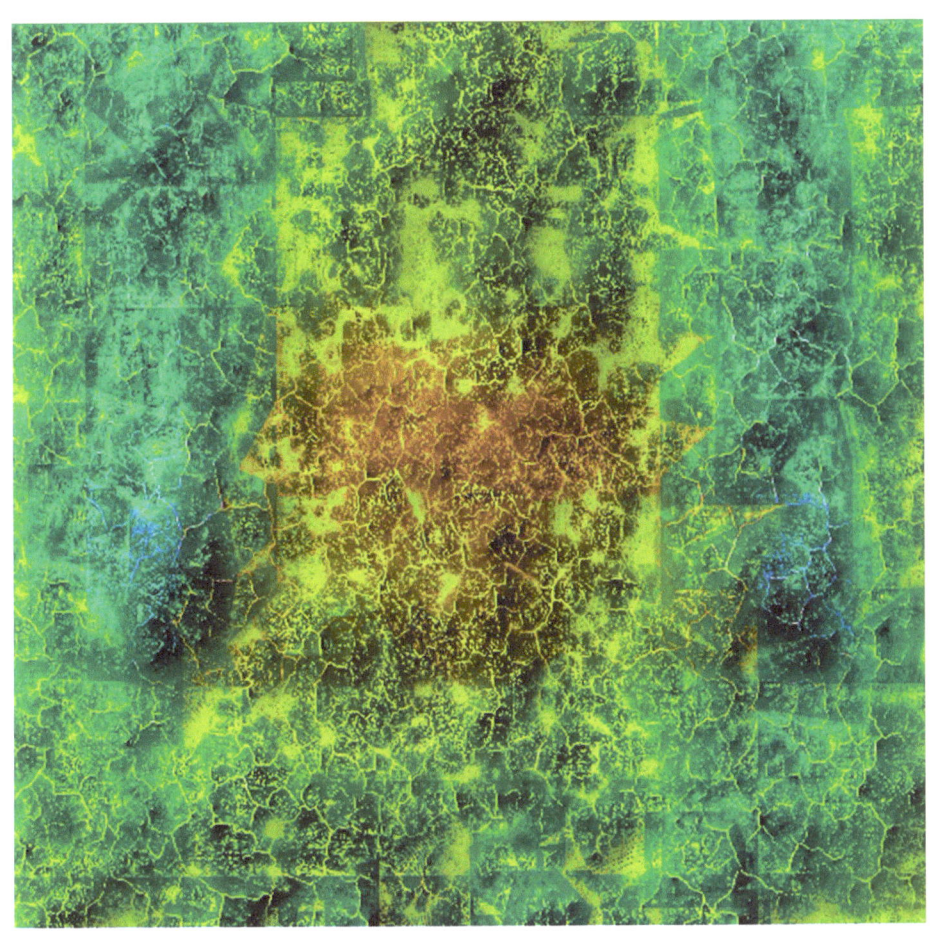

wake up and walk down

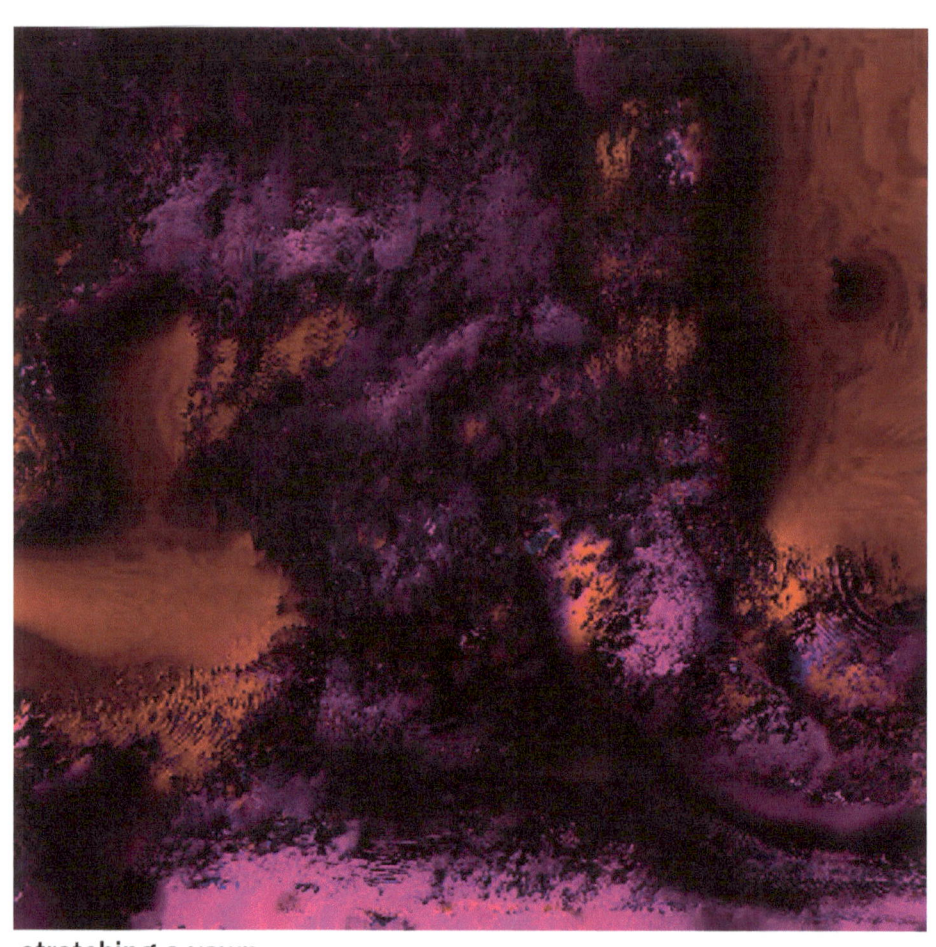

stretching a yawn

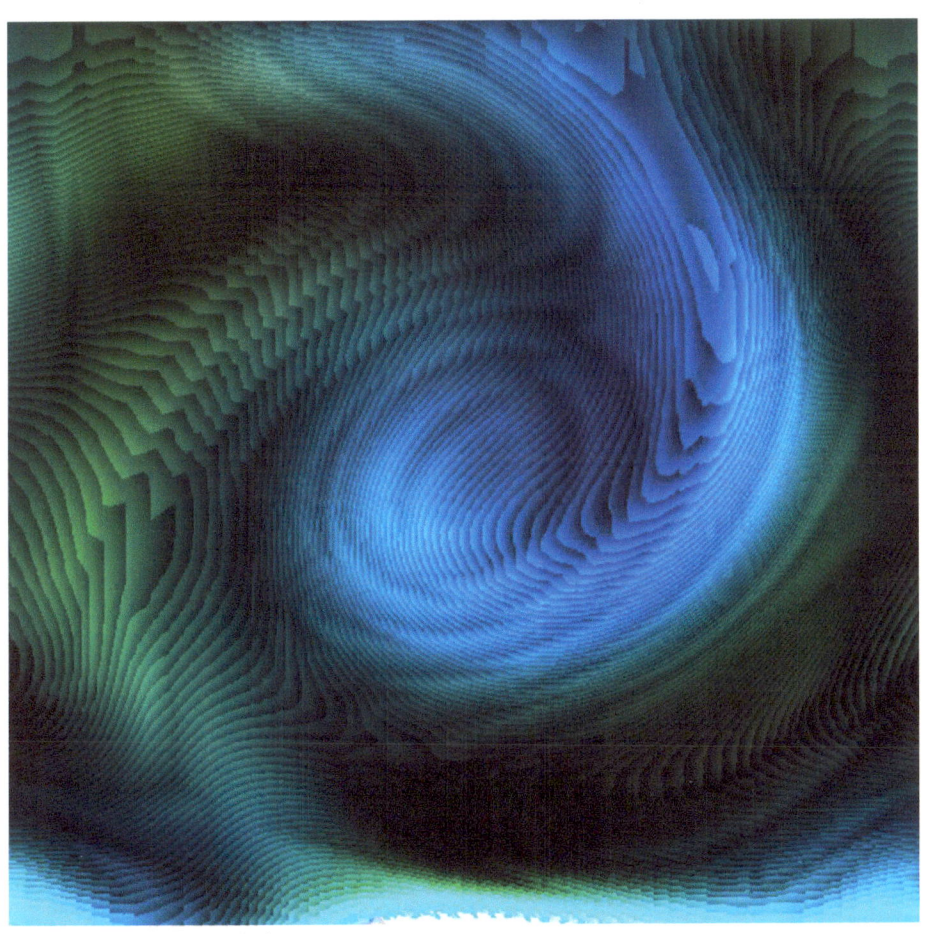

walk over to work it out

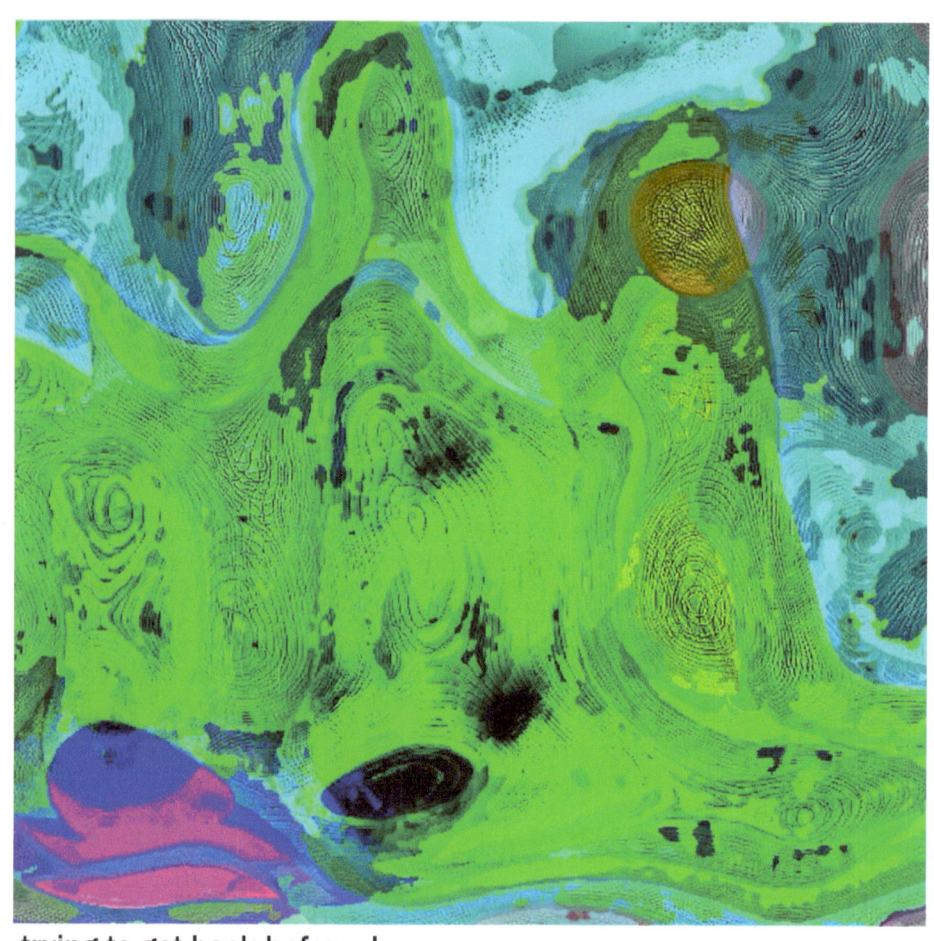

trying to get back before dawn

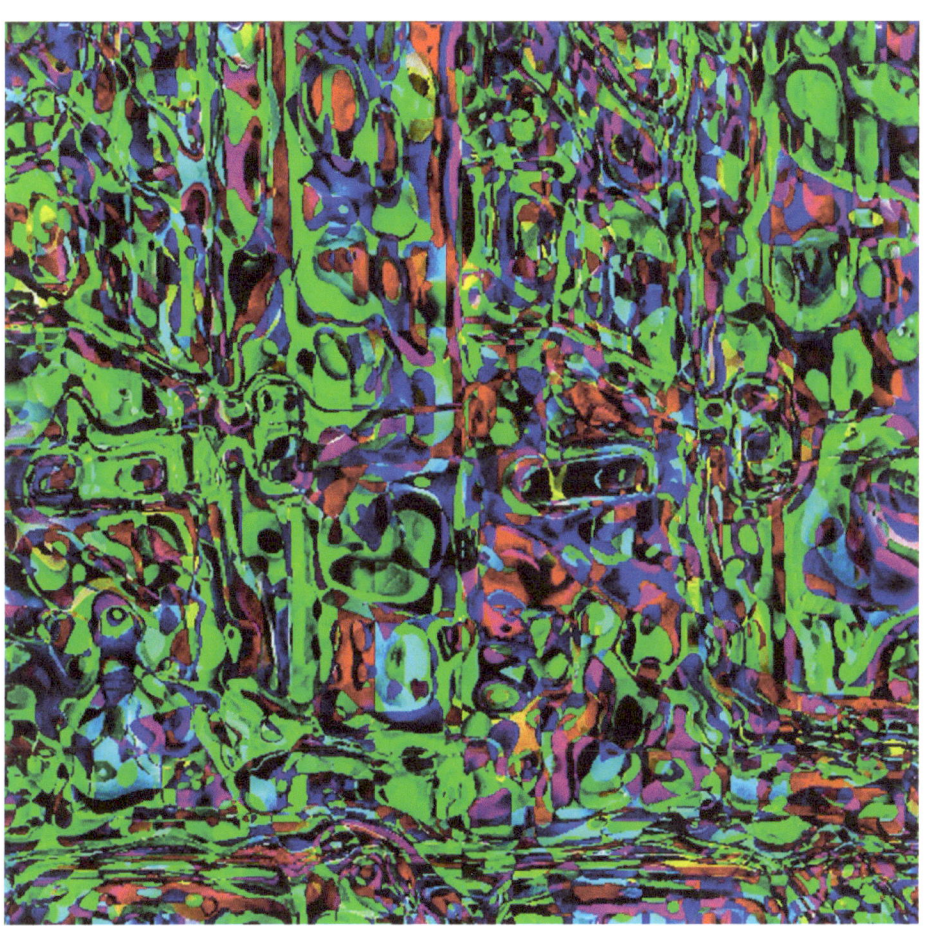

taking the short cut

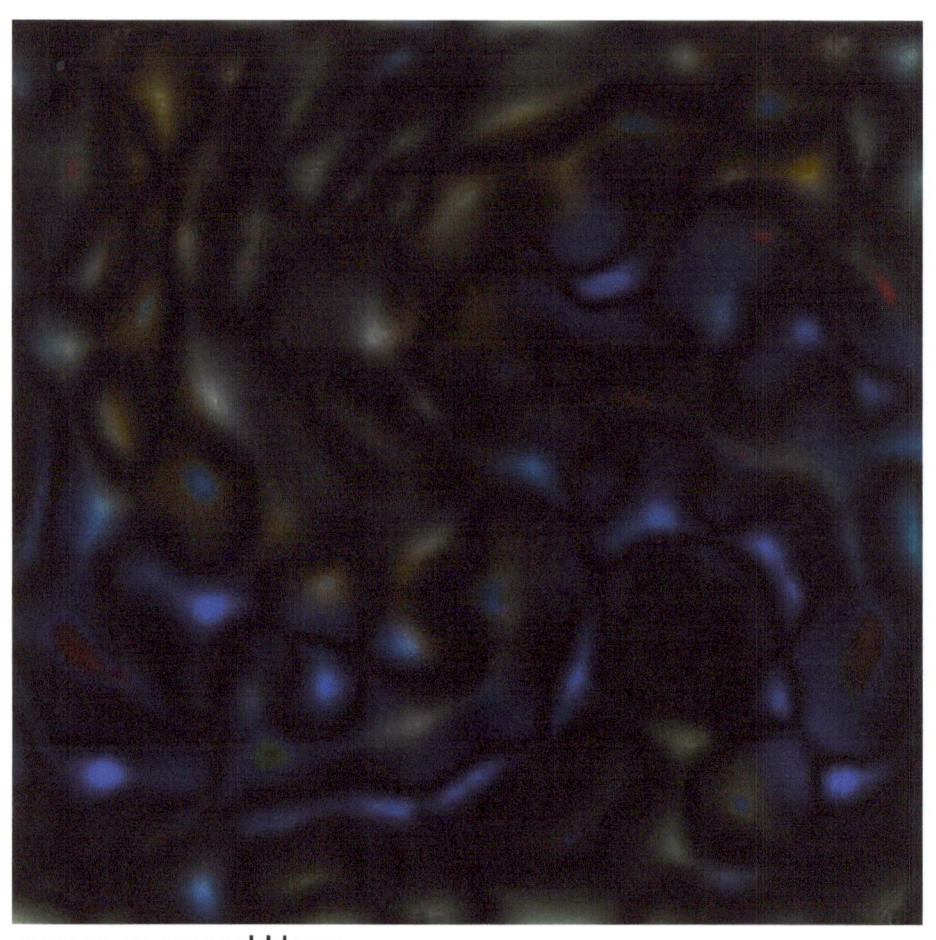

across an emerald lawn

through the palace

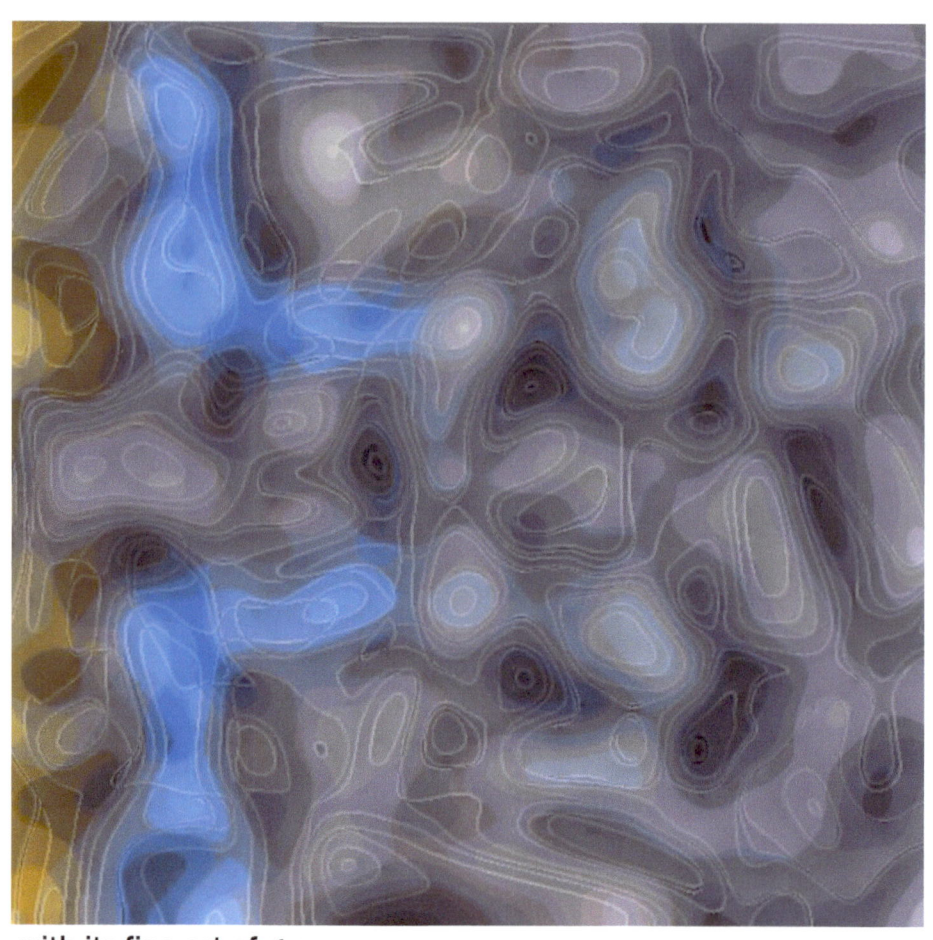

with its fine art of gone

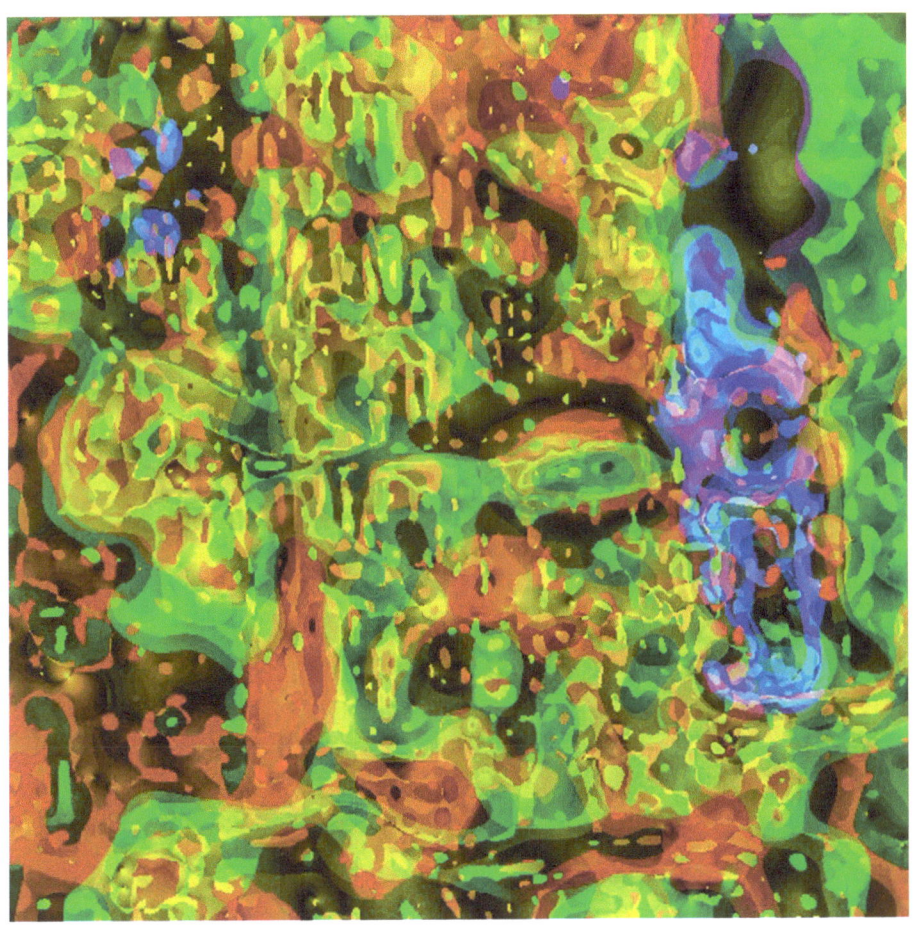

drawing out the monsters

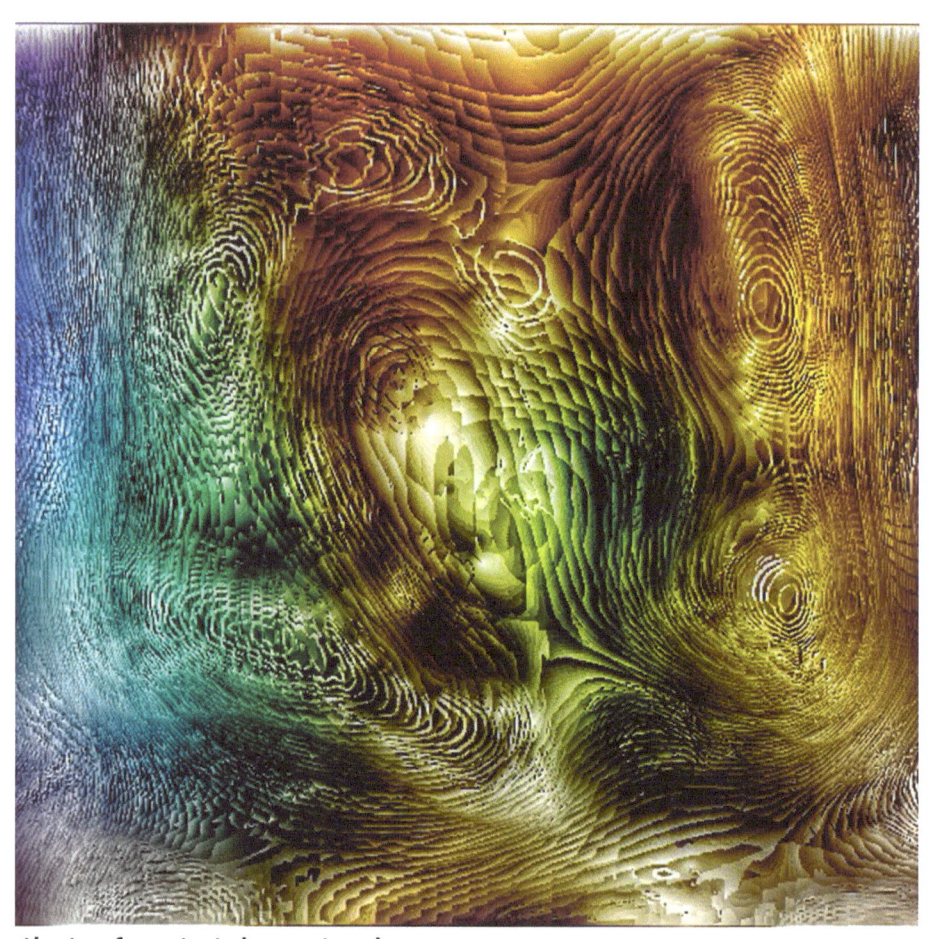

that refuse to take a stand

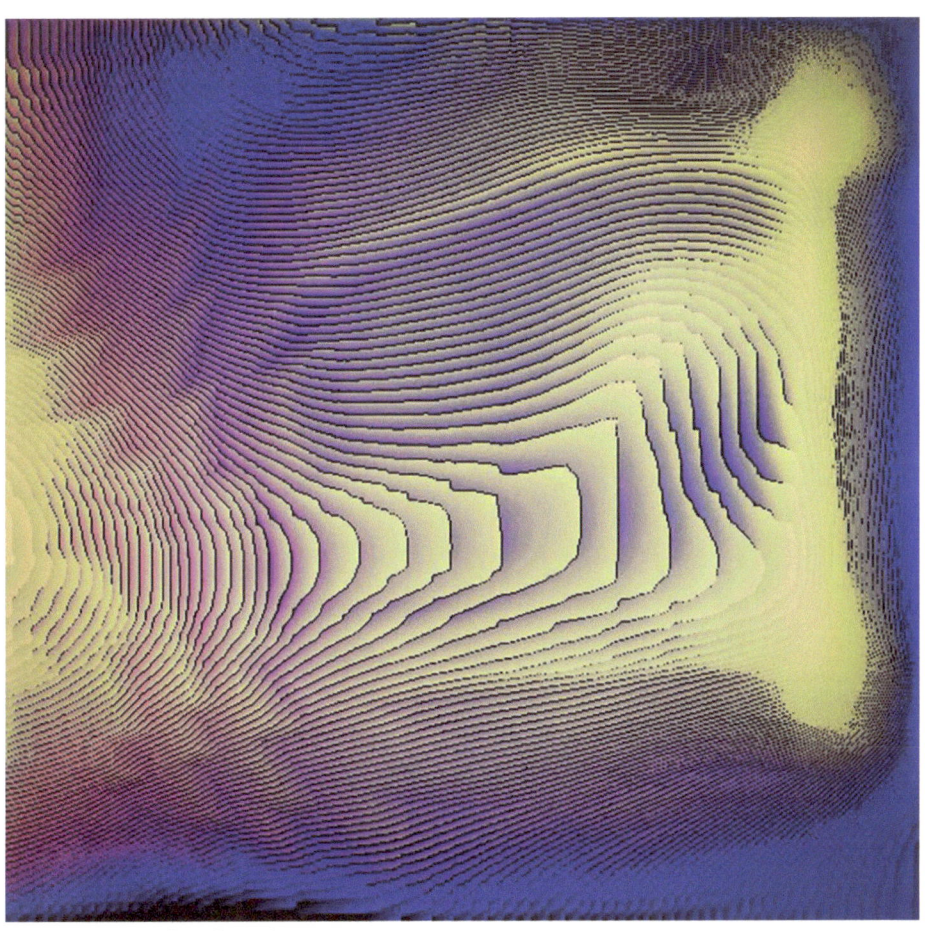

the curse of saint thomas

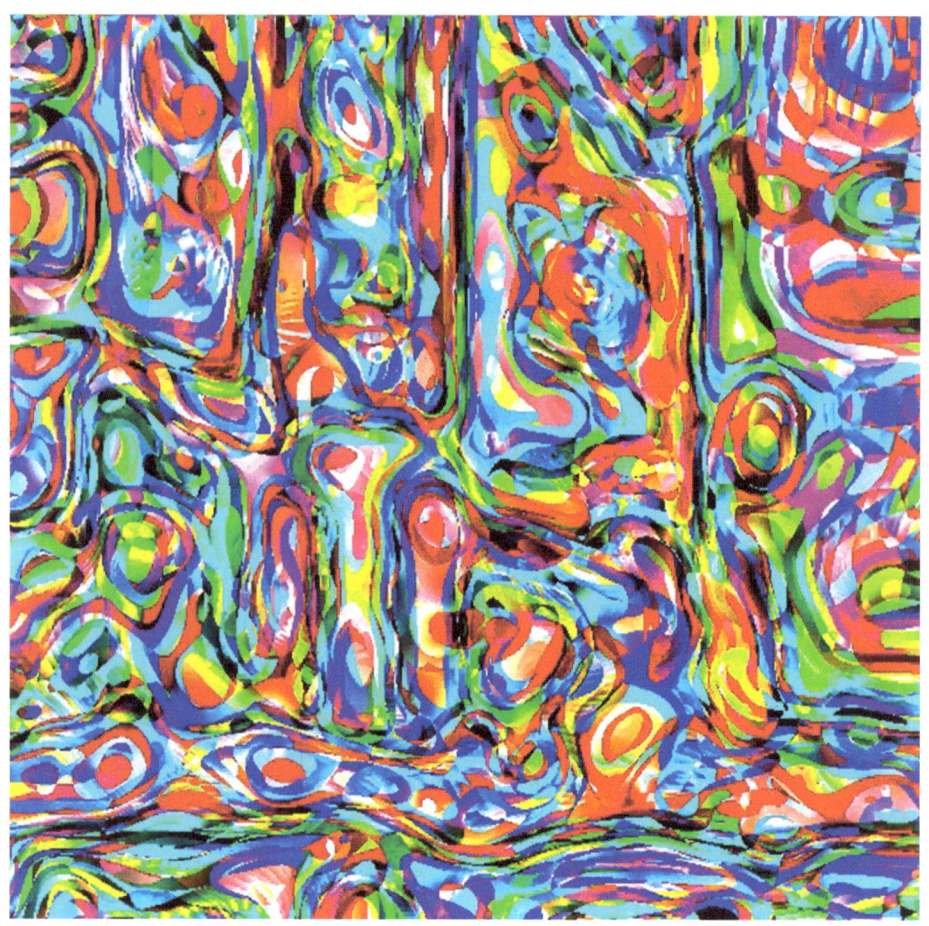

warning of a hide to be tanned

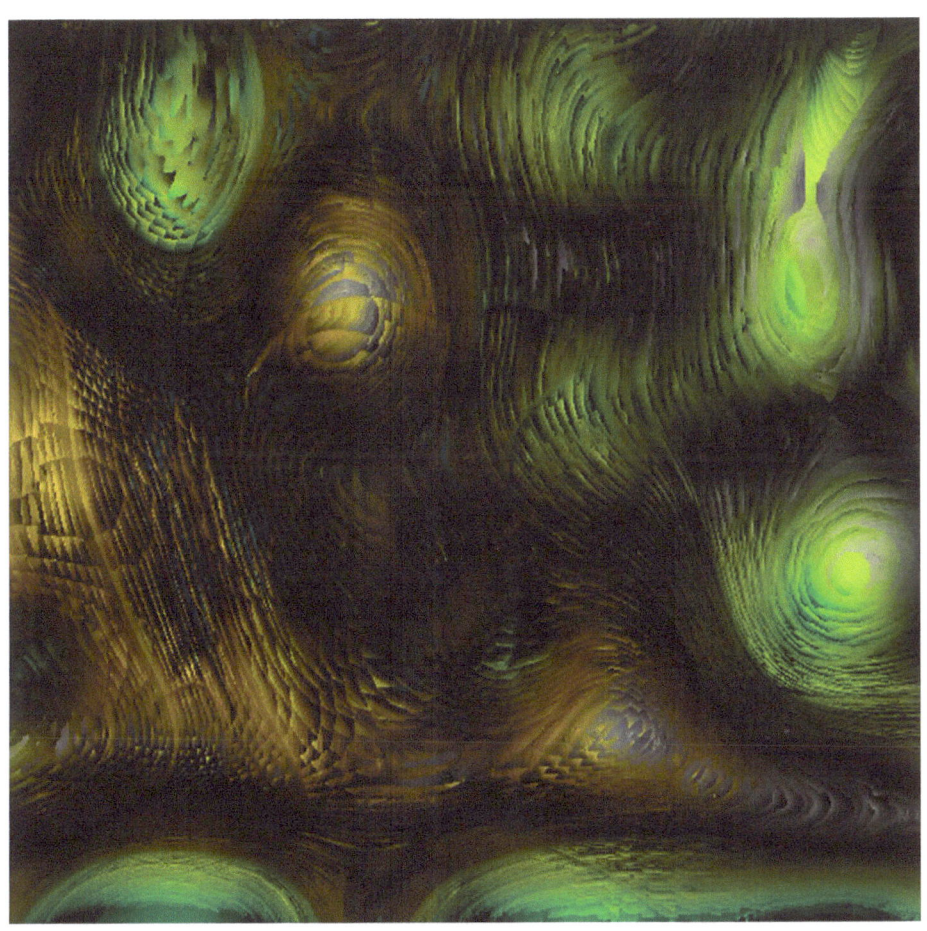

the prayer of saint joan

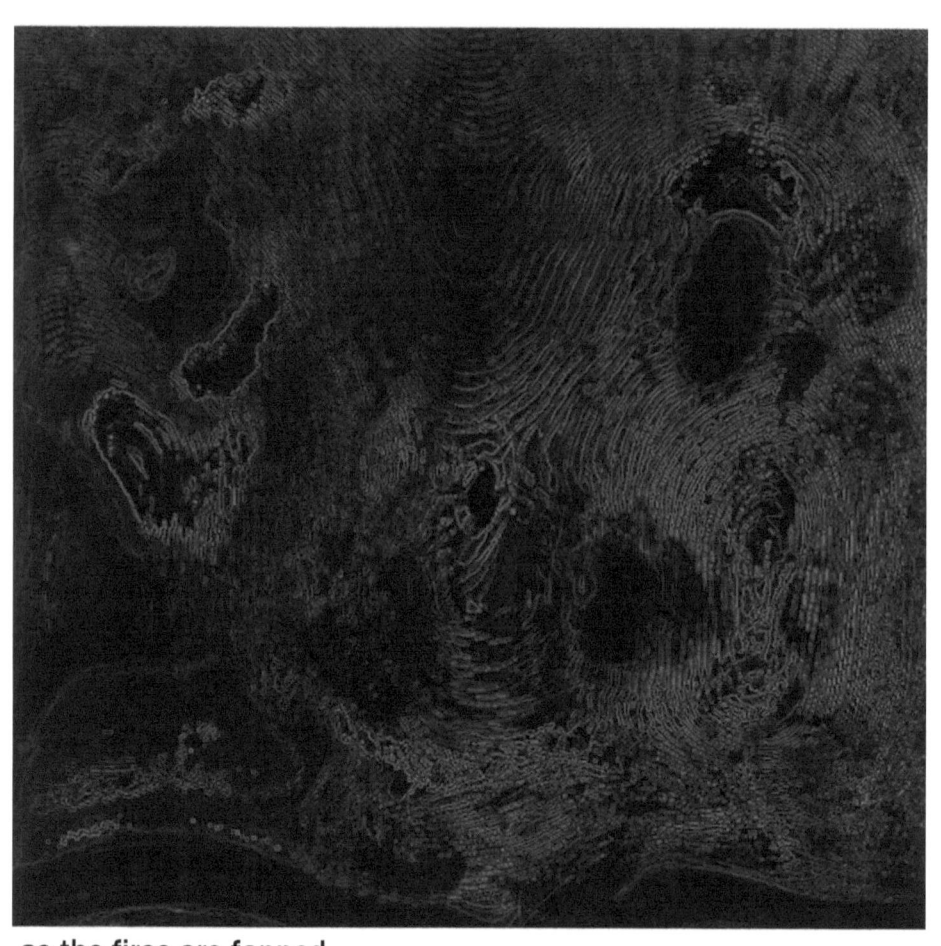

as the fires are fanned

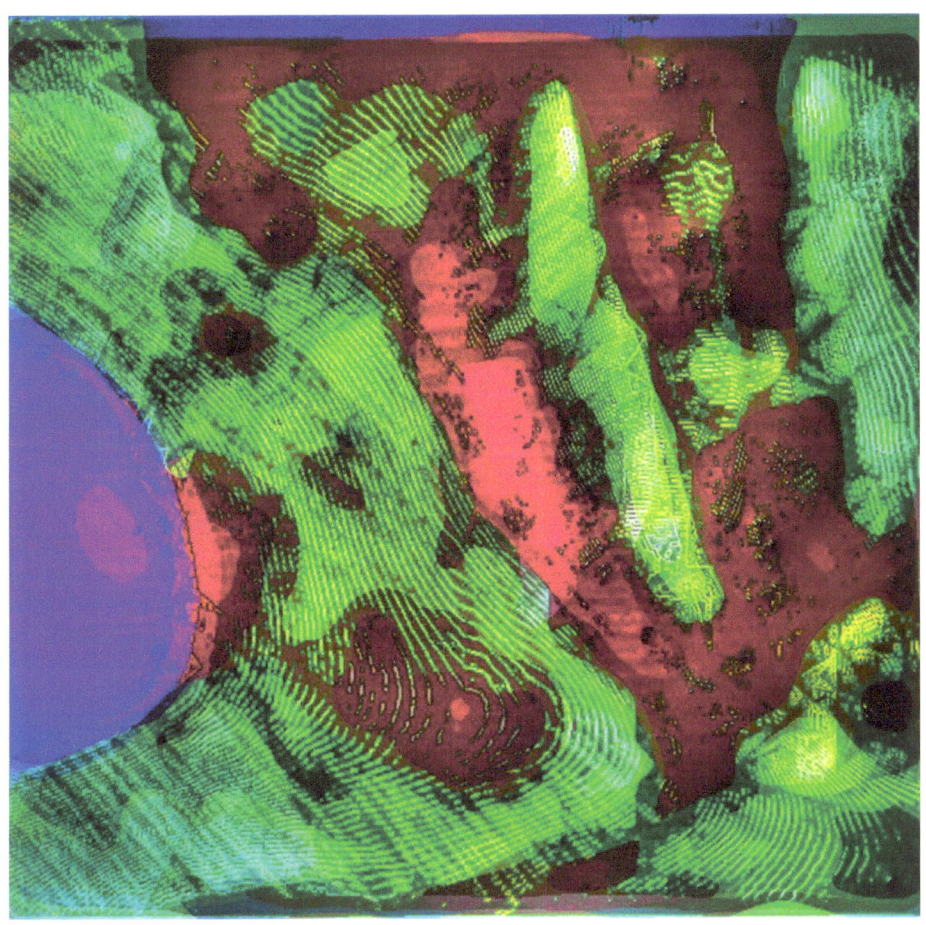

throwing it at the wall

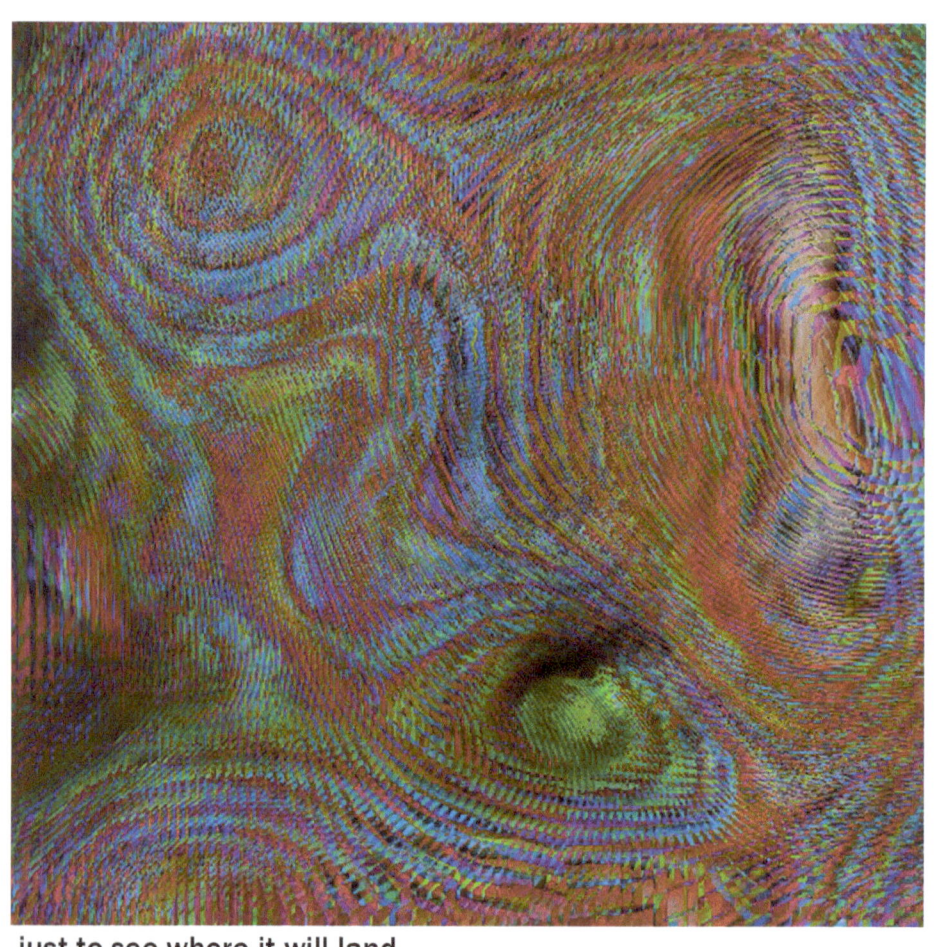

just to see where it will land

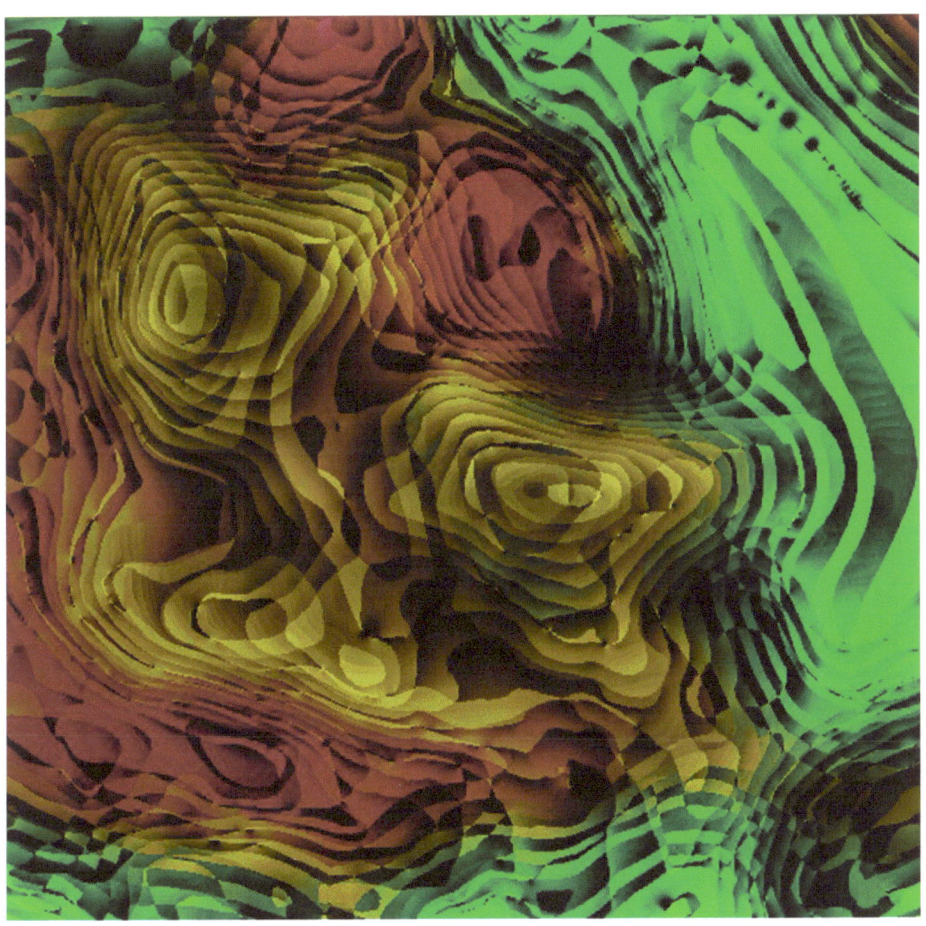

the moose and gorillas

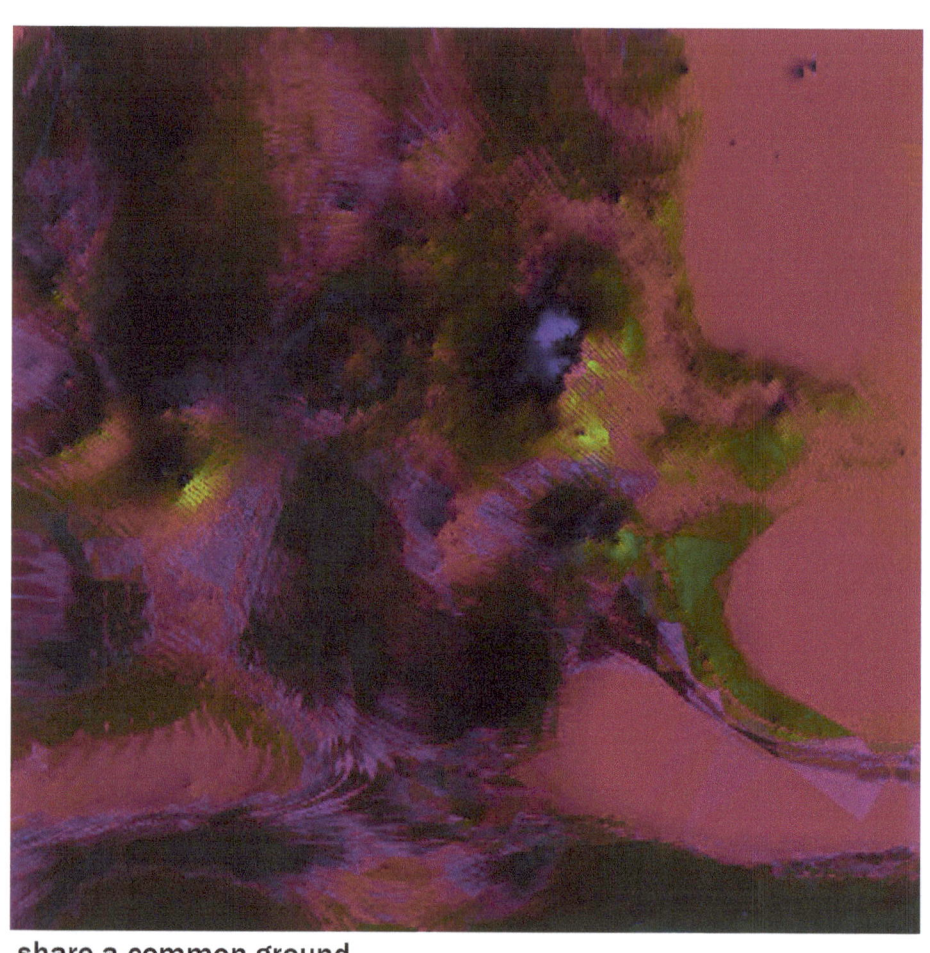

share a common ground

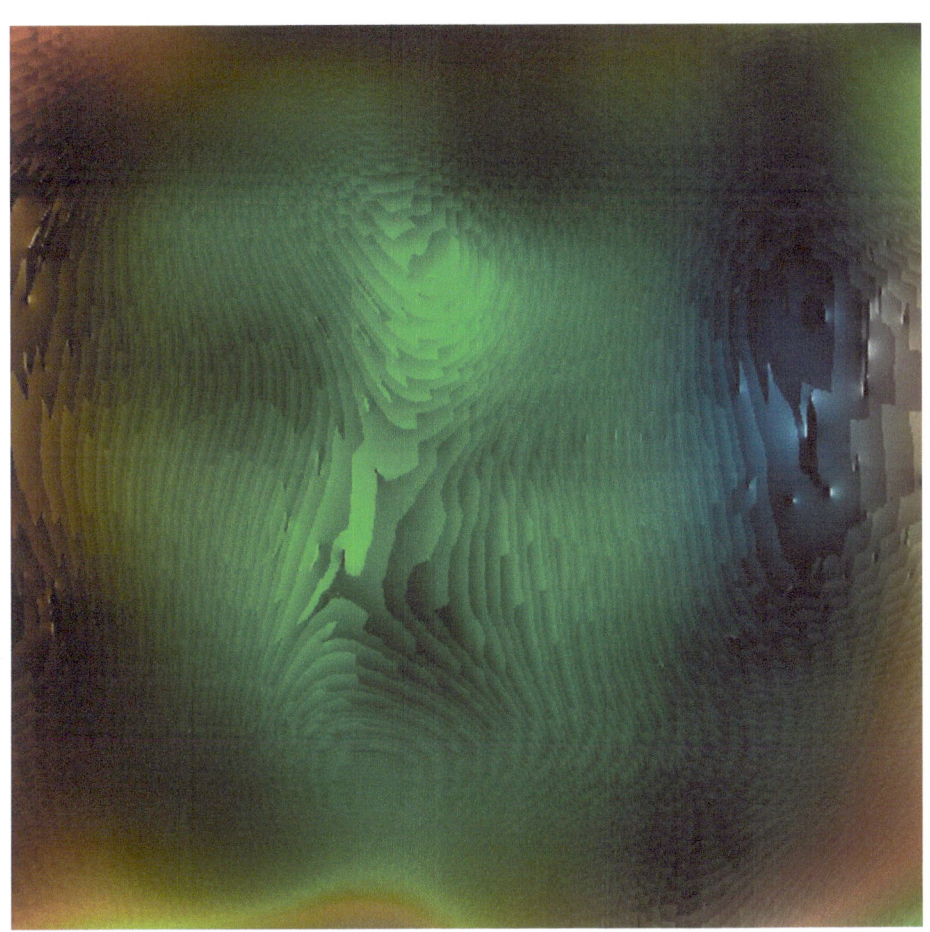

days of wet and smooth

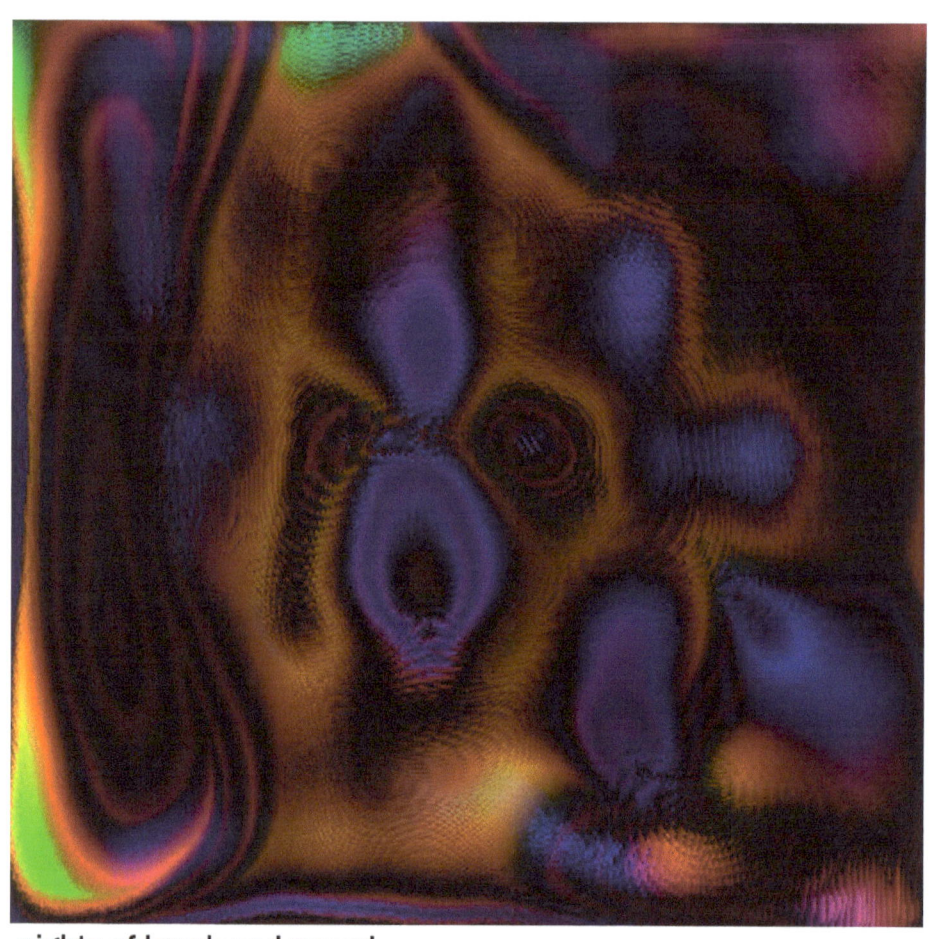

nights of break and pound

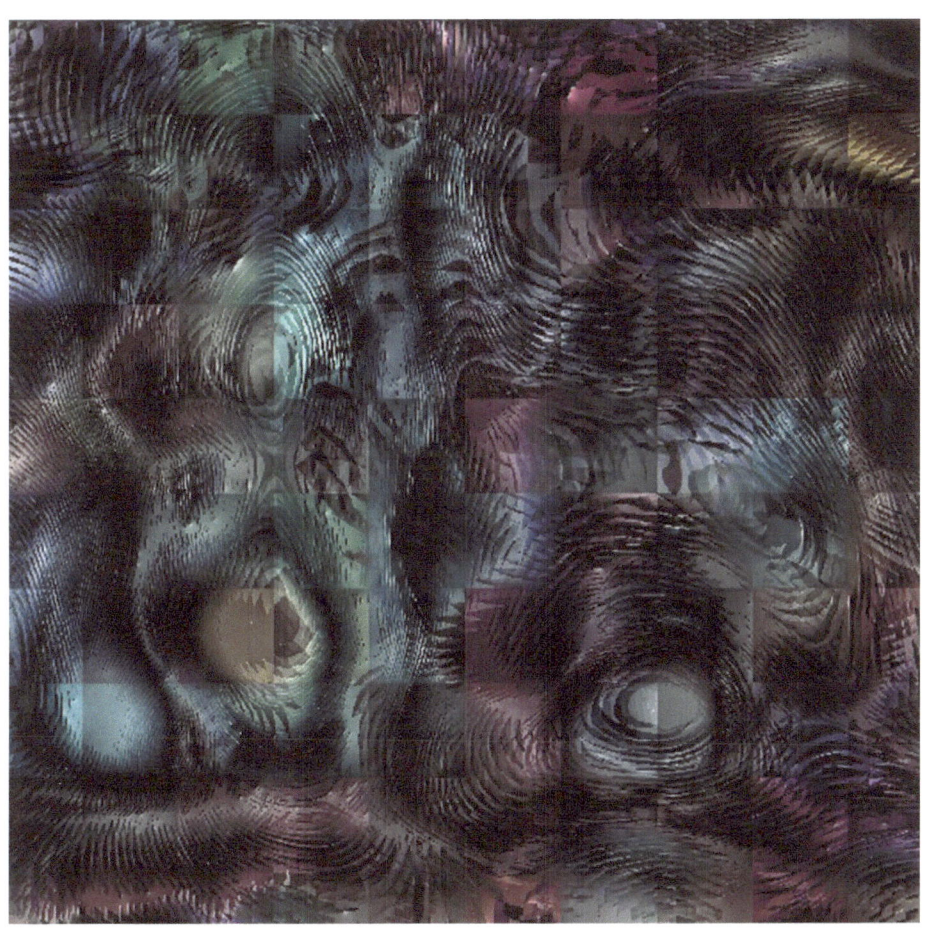

weeks of waiting

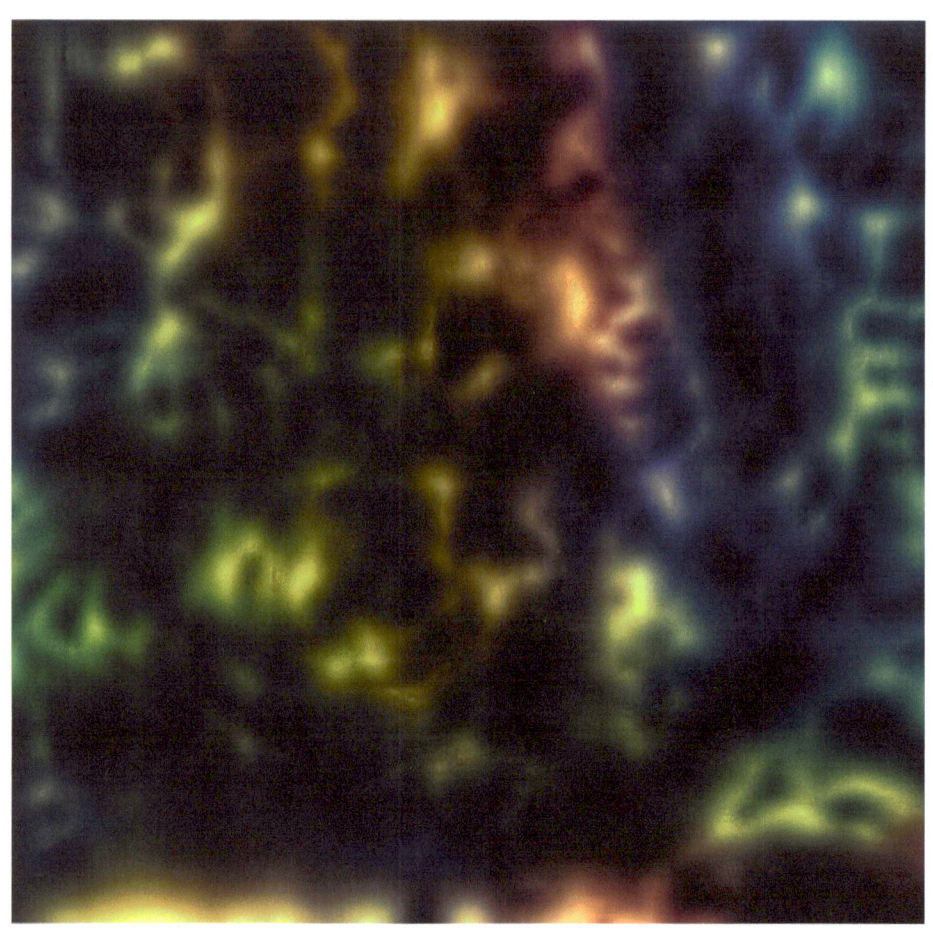

of missing sleep just to see

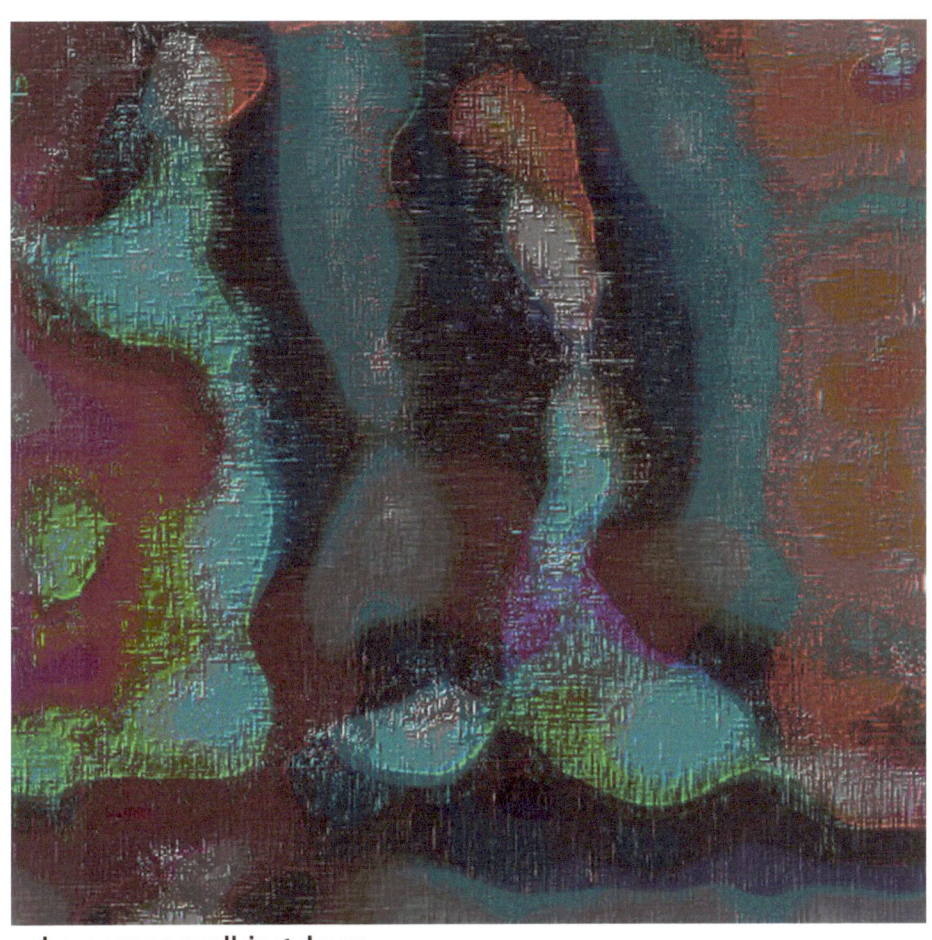

who comes walking down

www.ingramcontent.com/pod-product-compliance
Lightning Source LLC
Chambersburg PA
CBHW041622180526
45159CB00002BC/981